This Inspiration Belongs To:

Eleanor Pigg ♡♡♡

Write This for Inspiration

A Guided Journal for Getting the Most Out of Your Life

ASHLY PEREZ

CLARKSON POTTER/PUBLISHERS
NEW YORK

FOR
MY BEAN
AND MY
PARENTS

HELLO, AND CONGRATULATIONS ON PICKING UP THIS WORKBOOK!

To me, that means that you're ready to jump-start your life by way of inspiration—and, lucky for you, that's my favorite topic. My name is Ashly Perez, and I'm a TV writer, an artist, and an all-around creative. Perhaps you've read my first book, *Read This for Inspiration*, and you're ready to take this next step in discovering the inspirations in your life. Or maybe you have no idea what the heck I'm talking about, and you just want daily doses of motivation. Either way, I'm glad you're here because, no matter who you are, this is the workbook for you! Before I tell you what this workbook is, let me first tell you what it's not.

1. **IT'S NOT HOMEWORK.** This is not another task to add to your ever-growing to-do list. It's not meant to stress you out or add pressure to your day.

2. **IT'S NOT THE BE-ALL AND END-ALL ON INSPIRATION.** Think of this as another tool on your journey to discovering what brings meaning and joy to your life.

3. **IT'S NOT MINE, IT'S YOURS.** This is your space to use however you see fit. Inspiration, as you'll find out, isn't just one thing—it's whatever works for you. Flip through this workbook, and do ten pages, one page, or all of them at once—whatever makes you happy. There's no wrong way to use it, as long as it's working for you!

All right, now that we've gotten that out of the way, let's talk about what exactly this workbook is and why I wrote it.

Write This for Inspiration is exactly what it sounds like: it's a guide to finding the inspirations that are already present in your life and discovering new ways to find joy and motivation. **It's part journal, part workbook, and all safe space to take a minute and reflect on where you are in your life and where you want to go.** It is not meant for any particular job or profession, nor is it geared toward a particular type of person—because, frankly, there isn't anyone in the world who couldn't use a little inspiration now and then. It's an antidote to stagnancy and a seed of change. The root of the word "inspiration" comes from the Latin *inspirare*, which means "to breathe into." Inspiration breathes life into tired routines, shakes the sleeping self, and imbues us with energy. Does that sound like something you're looking for? Great, me too! Shall we?

When it comes to finding inspiration, the "why" part is easy—it's the "how" part that can get a little tricky. We've been taught to sit around and wait for inspiration to strike. That only the lucky feel energized. But that, my friends, is a big lie. Inspiration is not a waiting game, and it's not a lottery of luck. Instead, it requires active participation, because, in reality, inspiration is all around us, just waiting to be noticed. Mary Oliver put it best in her short poem "Instructions for Living a Life," in which she advised, "Pay attention. Be astonished. Tell about it." To me, that is the key to inspiration: not waiting for it to strike, but rather paying attention to the inspiration that already abounds. This workbook is an active guide to helping you pay attention. It is a space for you to acknowledge and respond to all the possibilities that are already in front of you. Your life deserves to be "breathed into." You deserve to be inspired.

Now, let's get down to the brass tacks.

HOW TO USE THIS WORKBOOK

Write This for Inspiration is a starting point. Use it as a tool to help you discover what's next. Whether you're feeling stuck in a tired routine, unsure of who you are, or just want to add some joy to your days, this is your space. The prompts are broken down into five categories: purpose, perspective, creativity, relationships, and empowerment.

"**Purpose**" asks you why you're where you are in your life and where you want to go. "**Perspective**" helps you shift the ways in which you see the world. "**Creativity**" allows you to get in touch with your artistic side. "**Relationships**" guides you toward building healthy connections and setting boundaries. And, finally, "**Empowerment**" creates space for you, because if you don't take care of yourself, you can't take care of others.

Let me put it to you this way . . . Want to get going on your career? Check out the prompts in "**Purpose.**" Seeking a refresh in your friendships? Look to "**Relationships.**" Want a taste of the different ideas the world has to offer? Then "**Perspective**" is for you. You see where I'm going with this? You design your own adventure. Remember, the most important rule of this book is that there are none!

Each of the entries, no matter the section, will encourage a different skill. Some are writing, some are illustrating (don't be intimidated–I, too, am terrible at drawing), and some are simply quotes, poems, and thoughts to be reflected upon. Though I encourage you to write and journal in this workbook, at the end of the day, it's not about "accomplishing" something; it's about granting yourself the time and space for self-discovery. You are valuable because you *exist*, not because you *do*. Remember that by simply being here and giving yourself time to pay attention, you are one step closer to inspiration. And with that, my friends, the world is your oyster. Or, at least, this workbook is!

PURPO

SE

IN MY EXPERIENCE, the big questions we all ask ourselves (*What is my purpose in life? Why am I here? What am I supposed to do next?*) are impossible to answer without pausing and finding space for rediscovery. Use this section to take a moment to wade through everything you've been told you are. Rediscover your core self, examine where you are in your life right now, where you spend your time, and set meaningful intentions for your future.

THINK LIKE A KID. You may find yourself wondering, *What should I do with my life?* The key is often in the past. My girlfriend always says that the core of adulthood is learning to unabashedly love the things that made you happy when you were eight years old. Make a list of your seven favorite things you did as a kid.

running as fast as possible

daisy chains

play music on radio and dance

bike

FATHERLY ADVICE

Advice I often turn back to in times of doubt is the advice Diane Sawyer's father gave to her: "Do something you really love in the most adventurous place you can, and make sure it helps other people."

Does your life reflect this advice? If not, what can you change to make it a reality?

WHAT AM I SPENDING MY TIME ON? One of the pitfalls of creativity and productivity is shallow work. In an attempt to accomplish all of our goals at once, we accomplish none of them. Create pie charts using the circles below to help clarify how you might be spreading your energy too thin. Fill in the chart below with the five things you currently spend most of your time on. Use these questions to think about what you actually want to be spending time on. **What is taking up most of my energy?**

Is what I'm spending my time on the most important thing to me? ***What should I be focusing on instead?*** Now fill in this chart to represent the five things you *actually* want to be spending time on. They can be the same five things from the first chart, divided differently, or they can be entirely new things!

BELIEVE IN YOURSELF. My Tía Esther always says that in order to write something, you have to believe it. What is a truth you believe about yourself?

I believe that I . . .

YOU'RE NEVER TOO OLD. Lucille Ball was forty years old when the first episode of *I Love Lucy* premiered. She had been told that she was too old, past her prime, and would never be a star. What is something that you secretly feel you are too old to start? Now, go do it!

DO YOU.

What's something you stopped doing because someone told you it wasn't cool? Write down an action plan for getting back into your happy hobby.

FIRST STEPS FIRST.

We're often taught to think in big leaps. Where do you see yourself in five years? What's your ten-year plan? All you really need to move forward, though, is the first step. Let's break it down.

WHAT IS YOUR GOAL FOR THE WEEK?

WHAT IS THE FIRST STEP TOWARD THAT GOAL?

GREAT JOB!

Even writing down the first step is a huge achievement—you're on your way!

BOOK. CHAPTER. VERSE. Sometimes it's hard to see the forest for the trees. Throughout their lifelong friendship, Oprah Winfrey and Gayle King developed a shorthand for this: a framework they use to talk about where they are in the story of their lives: book, chapter, verse.

Try using the same framework to help clarify where you are and where you're headed in the hypothetical story of your life. For example: "Book" might be "my twenties." "Chapter" might be "Am I doing what I love?" And "verse" might be "Should I quit my job, or stay longer to get more work experience?"

BOOK:

CHAPTER:

VERSE:

The Declaration of You.

Take out the "aspiring" disclaimer that sits before your goals. Aspiring writer. Aspiring chef. Aspiring activist. Aspiring mother. Aspiring rock climber. Write your truth.

I, ____,

[your name]

am a / an ______________________________________

GEEK OUT. It has been said that to find your passion, you must follow your bliss. I like to think of it in terms of "geeking out." That is, what do you love so much that, when you start talking about it, you get so excited you can't stop? For me, it's queer couples on television, etymology, and rom-coms. What is it that lights your heart on fire? How can you add more of that to your life?

WHO WOULD YOU HELP? Sometimes I like to envisage who I would help if all my dreams came true. If all of yours did, what foundation or volunteer organization would you start?

YOUR DREAMS CAN BE ABOUT PEOPLE AND THINGS OUTSIDE YOURSELF. KEEP DREAMING!

Bloom

Bloom at
your own pace.
Flowers bloom
in their own time.
They bloom when
they're ready, not
because the flower
next to them is
blooming.

What is a place in your life where you are rushing your growth because you're comparing yourself to others?

THE IN-BETWEEN SPACES.

It can be hard when you feel like you don't fit in any one box. But the space between boxes can be just as beautiful and feel just as good. Fill in the Venn diagram below, and celebrate the intersections of yourself.

These can include your race(s), sexuality, goals, interests—whatever makes you, you.

Invisible dream

There is a dream trapped
inside my head
The people who get me
can see the invisible dream
The others cross their eyes
squint
and pretend to see

TRANSITIONS. We are always changing and growing. The root of the word "transition" comes from the Latin word *transire*, which means "to go across." What two places are you straddling? In which direction do you see yourself growing?

SELF-MADE HANG-UPS. One of the most freeing experiences of my life was dyeing my hair blond at thirty years old. I always told myself, "You're not the type of girl that dyes her hair," and then one day, I just finally did it. It reminded me that so many of our insecurities and hang-ups are actually of our own making. What is a rule you've made for yourself that is holding you back?

CHOOSE YOUR OWN DESTINY

WHAT IS YOUR CALLING? If you don't know, don't worry! Use this space to write down the things you want to explore or learn more about.

THE ANSWERS

The key to moving forward in your life, career, and relationships is having the courage to ask the questions you need answers to. Write down five unanswered questions that are taking up a lot of your mental space.

“and” not “either”

Life isn't binary. The beauty of humanity is the ability to be so many things at once. What are some either/or statements you can change into “ands”?

TURN THIS:

I am either ______________________________

or ______________________________.

INTO THIS:

I am ______________________________

and ______________________________.

TURN THIS:

I am either ______________________________

or ______________________________.

INTO THIS:

I am ______________________________

and ______________________________.

YOU'RE STUCK

MOVE

MOVE

WHEN

YOU'RE

STUCK

WHEN

STUCK. Some of the most valuable life lessons we learn come from times we've felt stuck in jobs or relationships. List three moments in your life when you've felt stuck and the lessons you've learned from them.

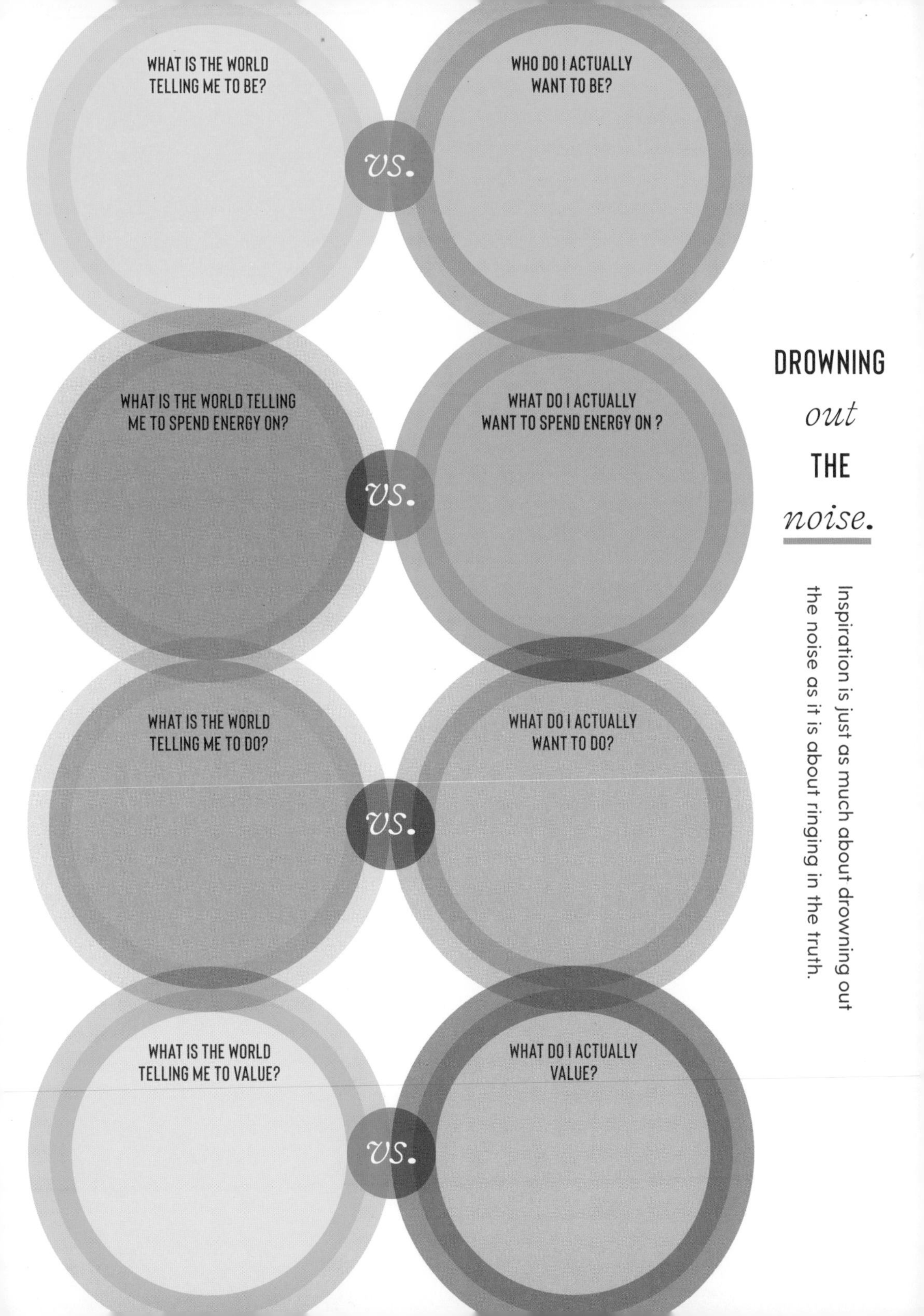
WHAT IS THE WORLD TELLING ME TO BE?
vs.
WHO DO I ACTUALLY WANT TO BE?
WHAT IS THE WORLD TELLING ME TO SPEND ENERGY ON?
vs.
WHAT DO I ACTUALLY WANT TO SPEND ENERGY ON ?
WHAT IS THE WORLD TELLING ME TO DO?
vs.
WHAT DO I ACTUALLY WANT TO DO?
WHAT IS THE WORLD TELLING ME TO VALUE?
vs.
WHAT DO I ACTUALLY VALUE?
DROWNING *out* THE *noise*.
Inspiration is just as much about drowning out the noise as it is about ringing in the truth.

WHERE PASSION MEETS PURPOSE

Finding your purpose is about finding the intersection between what impassions you and what you wish there was more of in the world.

What do you want to see more of?

How can you help?

FIGHT THE BIG FIGHT. Barbara Walters's advice to young women in *Oprah's Master Class* was "Fight the big fights, don't fight the little fight." What is the big fight in your life? What are the little fights you shouldn't spend time on?

DROP THE FEAR.

If you could do anything in the world right now, without the worry of responsibility, what would you do?

SUPERYOU. No matter what you've been told growing up, your superpowers are the things that make you different, not the things that make you the same as everybody else. List your four best superpowers.

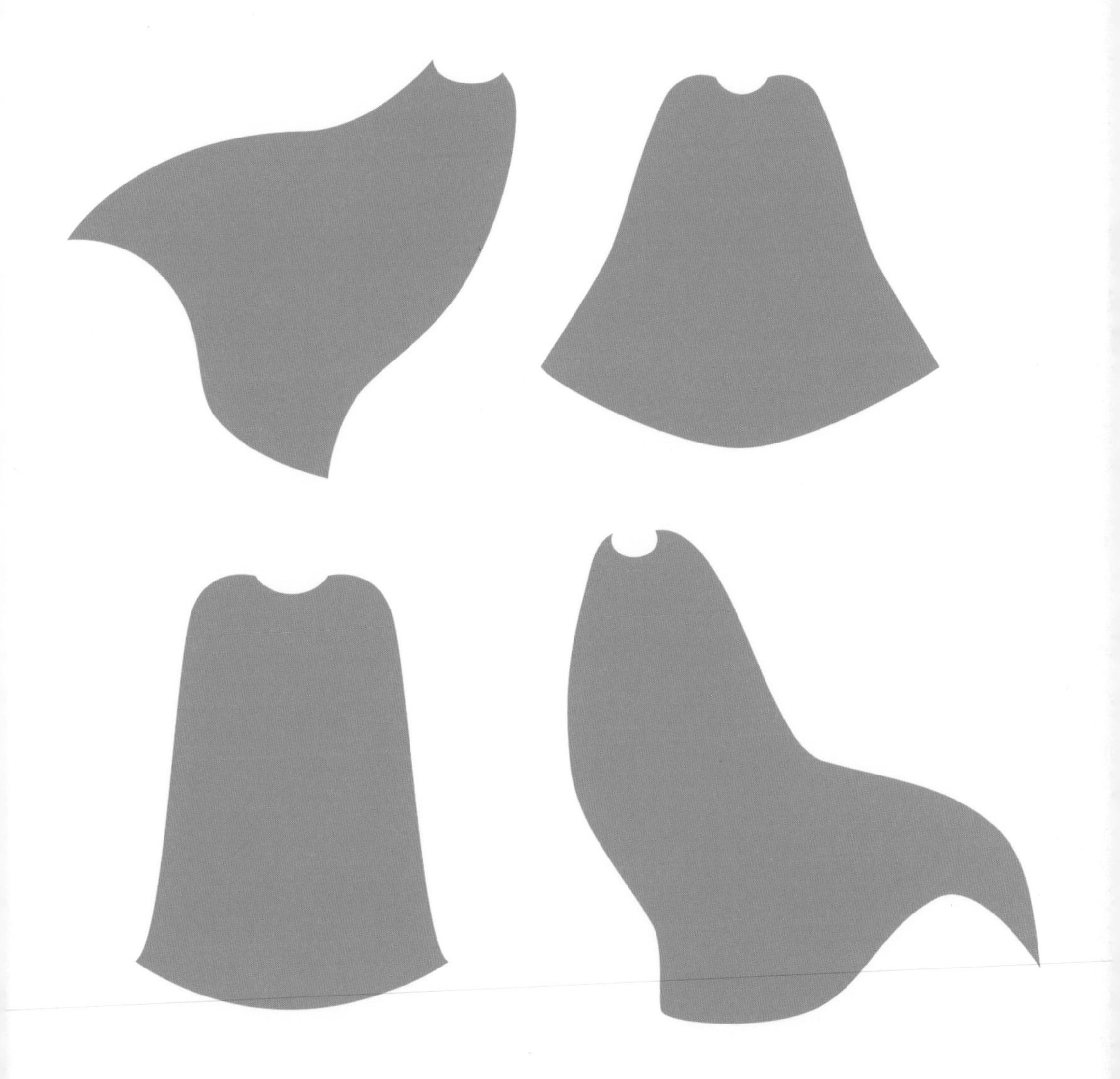

C O M P A

We only fall behind when we compare ourselves to others. We need to get away from "I'm not as ____________ as ____________"
[insert person]
statements and instead focus on ourselves.

WHAT ARE THE LIES YOU'VE BEEN TELLING YOURSELF?

I am not as ____________________

as ____________________.

I am not as ____________________

as ____________________.

I am not as ____________________

as ____________________.

Now, turn that around.

C O M P A

Remember that other people's lives and accomplishments have nothing to do with what you bring to the table.

I am valuable because ______________________________

____.

I am valuable because ______________________________

____.

I am valuable because ______________________________

____.

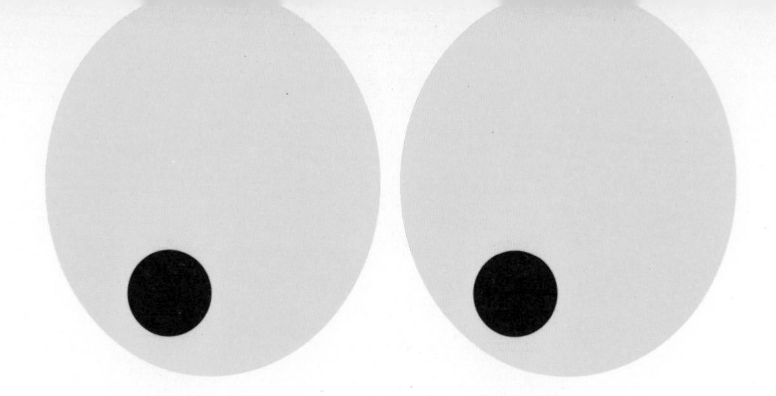

WHAT ARE YOU SO AFRAID OF?

Naming our fears helps us conquer them. We can't defeat what we refuse to acknowledge. Draw out your fears, and then doodle non-scary things on them (flowers, trees, bunnies) until they're not so scary anymore.

"The true meaning of courage is to be afraid, and then, with your knees knocking, to step out anyway."

–Oprah Winfrey

Where do you need to step out today?

HAVE

COURAGE

PERSP

ECTIVE

THE ROOT OF THE WORD "PERSPECTIVE" comes from the Latin *perspicere*, which means "to look through or see clearly." With a new perspective, we gain the ability to see ourselves more clearly. This section is about evaluating your perspective and finding new ones. Often, the easy path to change has nothing to do with our surroundings, but rather with how we interpret them. Use this section to challenge your current worldview and shift your outlook.

all these lives

There are all these lives in me,
some traveled,
unraveled,
some finished,
some never begun,
and yet each day I decide
who I would like to become.

UNLEARNING. A lot of growing into yourself is unlearning unhelpful lies. These could have come from your parents, your classmates, or society at large. What are three lies you grew up learning? Now, on the lines below, replace those lies with truths. (For example: I was told that brown girls weren't as pretty as white girls. Now I know the truth is that we all have beauty to bring to this world.)

LIES:

TRUTHS:

THA

GIV

Gratitude is the key to staying grounded, present, and appreciative for the life you have. You don't always need big changes to solve your problems—sometimes, all you need is a little push in the right direction. Write down three things you're thankful for today, this month, and in the last year.

NKS

ING

INSPIRATIONAL RETROSPECTIVE. Inspiration doesn't always have to be about discovering something new. Sometimes it can be about remembering the beautiful things that have already happened. Answer the first question, then close your eyes, reflect, and bask in those sensations before answering the next.

Where is the most beautiful place you've ever been?

What is a song that reminds you of a great time in your life?

Who in your life do you feel truly gets you?

When was the last time you felt carefree?

MORE THAN "SHOULD." There is power in turning your "shoulds" into "musts." Write three "shoulds" that you will turn into "musts" this month.

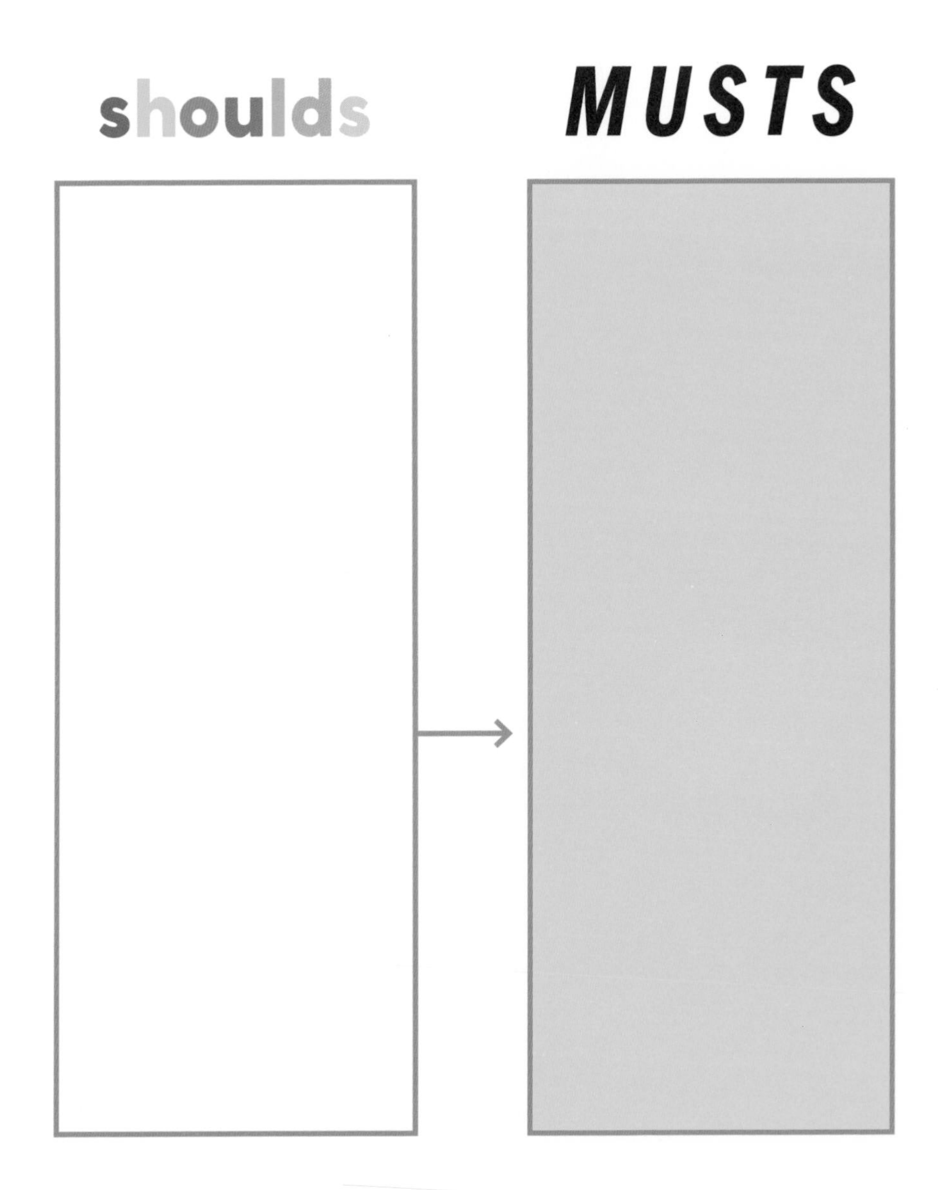

3

ON THE UP-AND-UP

2

When I feel stuck, I force myself to reflect on all the things I've learned lately. This could be a practical skill (like watercolor painting) or a personal lesson (like that saying no doesn't make me rude). Share three instances of what you've been learning lately and how those lessons have made you grow.

1

Making
for a

Just because it's a "no" doesn't mean it's a "never." Sometimes the "no" is simply clearing space for a better "yes" down the road. What was the most recent "no" you encountered? List at least one positive outcome from it.

My most recent "no"

space

→ YES.

→

P O S I T I V E O U T C O M E S

BLACK,
WHITE,

AND SOMEWHERE IN BETWEEN.

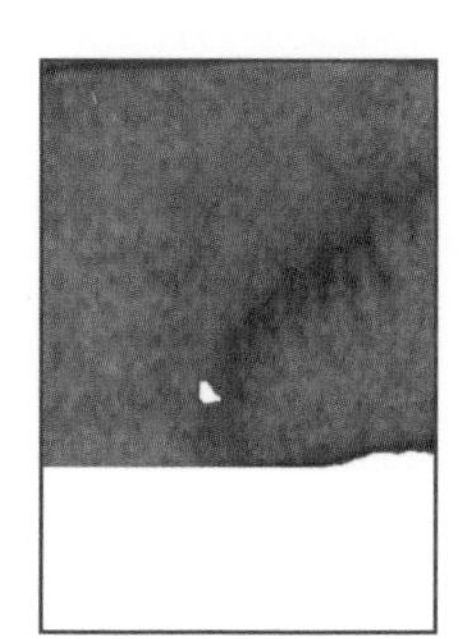

Bad to the bone

Running with the devil

Slightly sinful

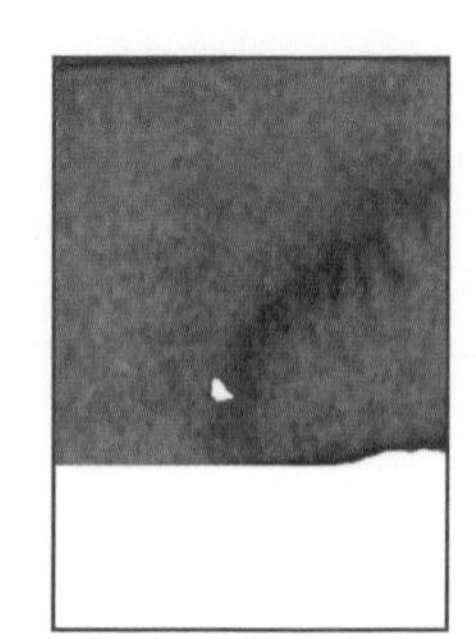

Some of the harshest judgments we'll ever receive are the judgments we give ourselves. We are trained to see things as black-and-white, when most of our traits are actually a shade of gray. Fill out your gray paint chips, and give yourself some leeway.

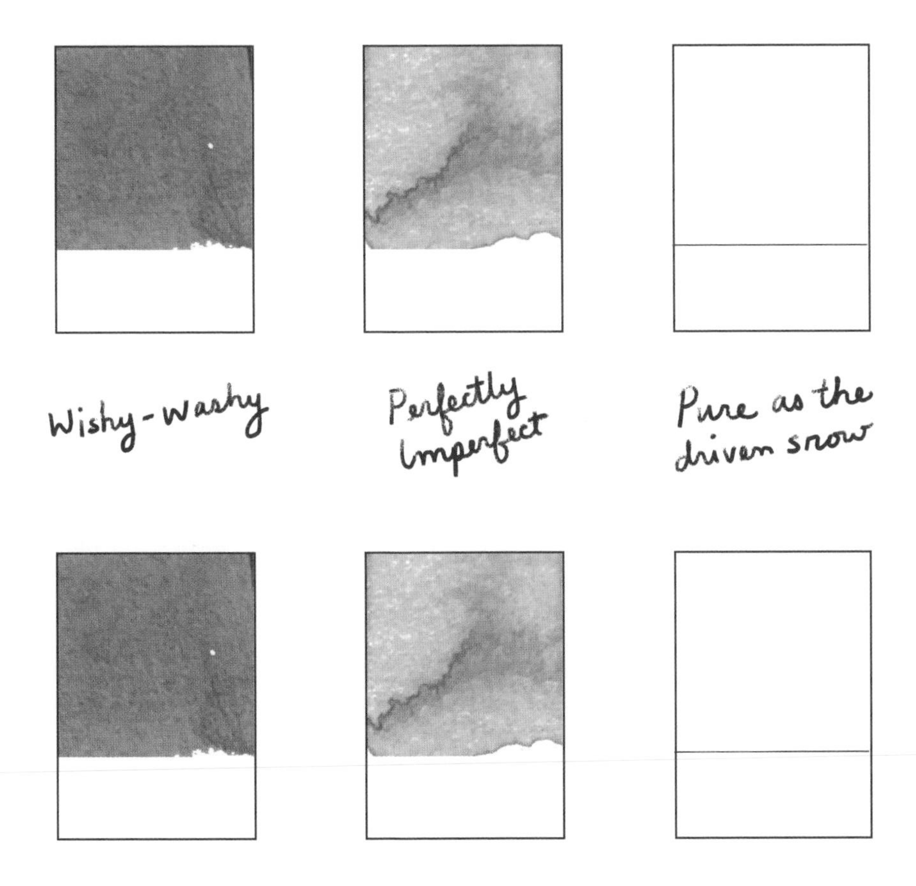

LITTLE **WINS.**

We sometimes operate on a winning binary—either we're winning or we're losing, with no in-between. But in my humble opinion, improving is winning. Making strides is winning. List your improvements for the week (for example: I meditated two days in a row. I kept the sink clear of dirty dishes.) As long as you are making strides toward your goals, it doesn't matter how significant they are. Celebrate! Fill in the medals with your little wins.

OLD WOUNDS. It's never too late to heal old wounds. What's something from your childhood that you need to resolve in order to move forward? How can you begin to resolve it?

ROADBLOCKS. Sometimes coming up against a wall on the way to our goals can help clarify what it is we truly want. What's a current roadblock in your life? Do you want to move past it and take this opportunity to head in a new direction?

IT'S OK TO NOT BE THERE YET

COLOR ME IN!

HUMAN *BEING*. We live in a society in which productivity is valued above most everything else. But that is a dangerous lie. You are valuable as a human because of your capacity to form connections with people and the world around you, not because you can check things off a to-do list. Write down some of the things you did today that had nothing to do with productivity.

The end is nothing

"The end is nothing:
the road is all."

—WILLA CATHER

WABI-SABI. In Japan, there is a design principle called wabi-sabi, and it dictates that what makes something beautiful are its imperfections. A desk worn with knicks and water stains is to be treasured because of its flaws, rather than in spite of them. What are some of your imperfections that you treasure?

WE ALL HAVE TRAUMA. In an interview with *Salon*, Nora Ephron said, "Almost nobody worth knowing has a happy childhood." In other words, our trauma can be an unconventional gift. Turn your trauma on its head, and write about the positive lessons you have learned from a hardship.

I've learned that we're all just trying our best, even when we mess up.

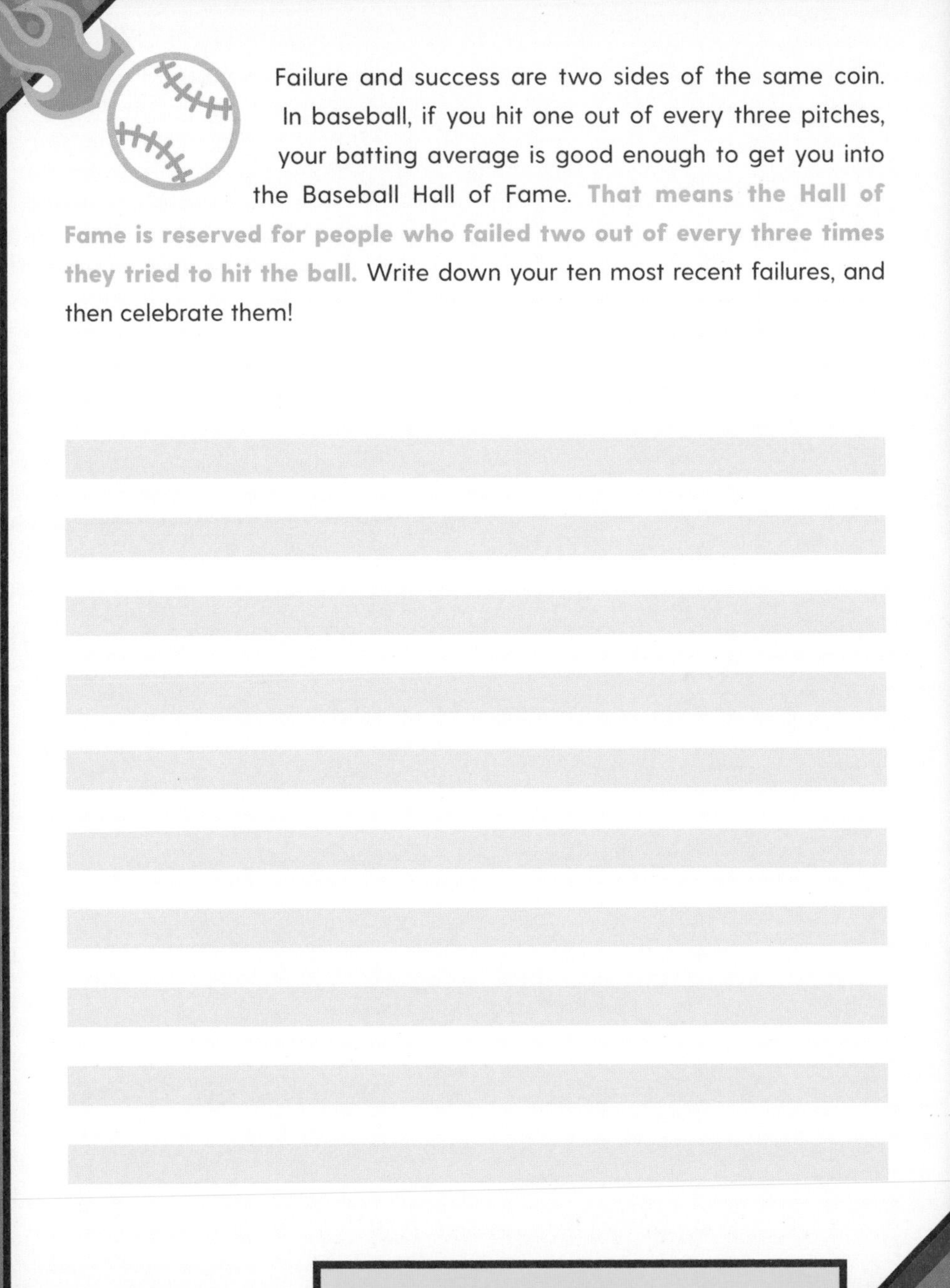

Failure and success are two sides of the same coin. In baseball, if you hit one out of every three pitches, your batting average is good enough to get you into the Baseball Hall of Fame. **That means the Hall of Fame is reserved for people who failed two out of every three times they tried to hit the ball.** Write down your ten most recent failures, and then celebrate them!

HALL OF FAILURE

ALL THIS NOTHING. One of my favorite movie lines is when Meg Ryan writes to Tom Hanks in *You've Got Mail* and says, "All this nothing has meant more to me than so many somethings." The best memories are the "nothings" found in between moments that are meant to mean "something." Celebrate your nothings. Write down three tiny moments of joy you experienced in the past month.

THE ENDING CYCLE. Oftentimes, our insecurities repeat like a broken record in our heads. A single negative thought can perpetuate the vicious circle of doubt. That's why we have to learn to interrupt our negative thoughts with one positive thought to break the cycle.

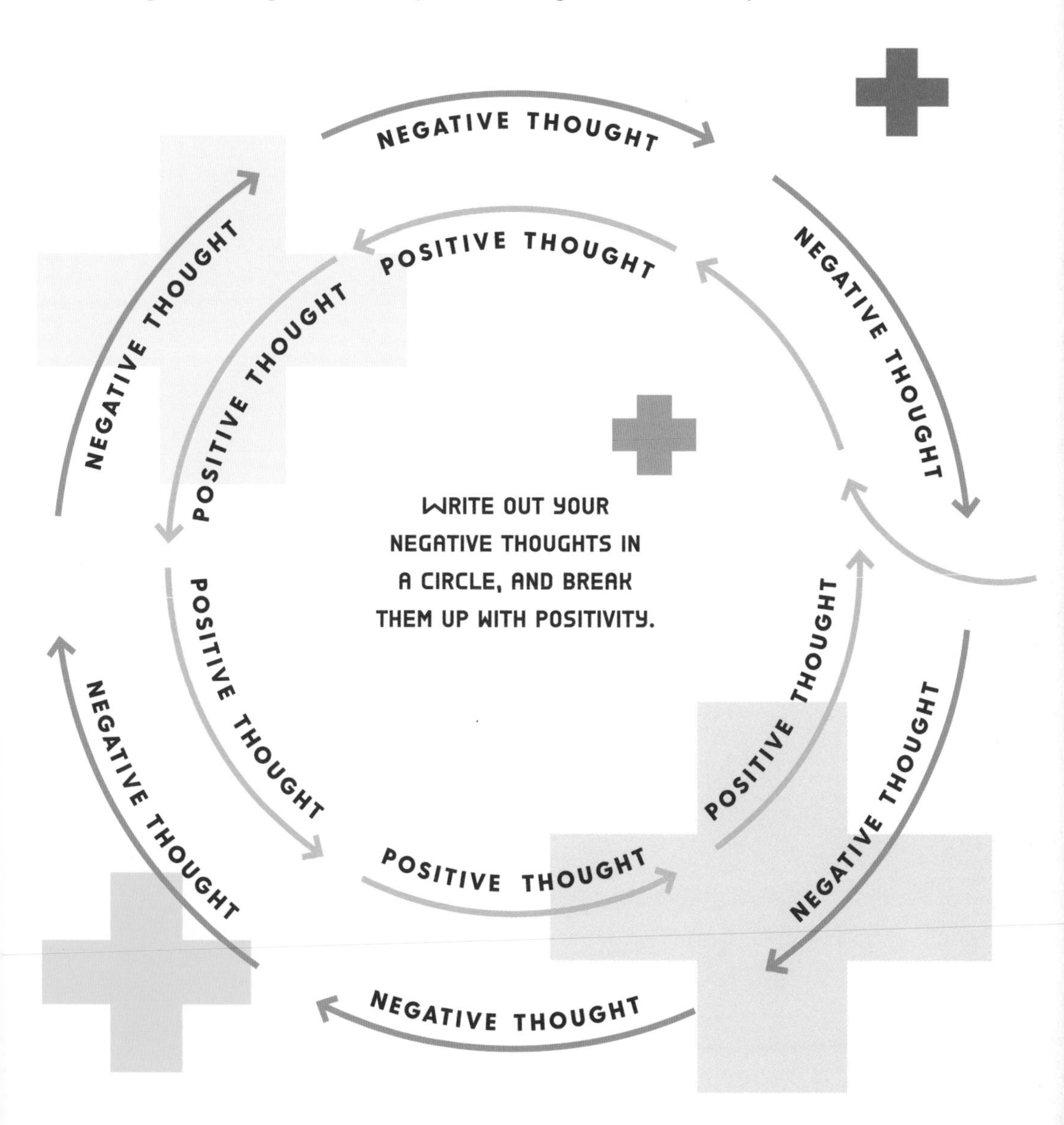

CONTENTMENT ★ ARROGANCE

DELIGHT ★ ECSTACY ★ FEAR

CURIOSITY ★ UNCERTAINTY ★ LETHARGY

BOREDOM ★ AMUSEMENT ★ CONFIDENCE

SURPRISING FEELINGS. Learning to identify your feelings is key to being able to understand where you are. Often, we bottle up all of our negative feelings in favor of positivity. But hiding your feelings isn't helpful; it's toxic. Circle the emotions you are feeling right now. Are you surprised by any of them? Have you been ignoring some of them? Why?

CREATIVITY ★ PAIN ★ TIRED

★ CONFIDENCE ★ EMBARASSMENT ★

★ SADNESS ★ OPTIMISM ★ GUILT

HAPPINESS ★ JEALOUSY ★ SICKNESS ★ ANGER

ANXIETY ★ GRATITUDE ★ WORRY ★

DON'T DWELL. It is good to reflect, but not to dwell. The root of the word "dwell" comes from the Old English *dwellan*, which means "to hinder or lead astray." What is something or someone you need to move on from? What or who is hindering your growth?

Dwellan

[verb]

OUT OF GOALS AND INTO GRATITUDE. At its core, inspiration is about appreciation. Write down ten things that you deeply appreciate in your life right now, and let them motivate you to move forward as well as stay present.

1. ______________________________

2. ______________________________

3. ______________________________

4. ______________________________

5. ______________________________

6. ______________________________

7. ______________________________

8. ______________________________

9. ______________________________

10. ______________________________

CR.EA
CR.EA
CR.EA
CR.EA
CR.EA

CREATIVITY IS NECESSARY

to living a full life, whether you consider yourself an artist or not. It is the manifestation of our inspiration. Use this section to get in touch with your inner Frida Kahlo. And remember: creativity isn't just about drawing or storytelling—there are lots of different ways to be creative.

DON'T *give up*

"Just don't give up trying to do
what you really want to do.
Where there is love and inspiration,
I don't think you can go wrong."

—ELLA FITZGERALD

Personally, whenever I'm feeling uninspired, I turn to my favorite playlist filled with the music I find most uplifting. Take a trip down memory lane, and make a list of five songs that always put you in a good mood and the memories they remind you of.

TITLE	MEMORY

MORNING PAGES. In her book *The Artist's Way*, Julia Cameron says that the best way to clear space for creativity is to start each morning by writing a three-page brain dump that will get all of the gunk and worry out of your head. Practice doing a set of morning pages. Freewrite for three pages, first thing in the morning (yes, you can get coffee or walk your dog first). You can write absolutely anything (a grocery list, stream of consciousness, dream journal, etc.), but it has to be three pages.

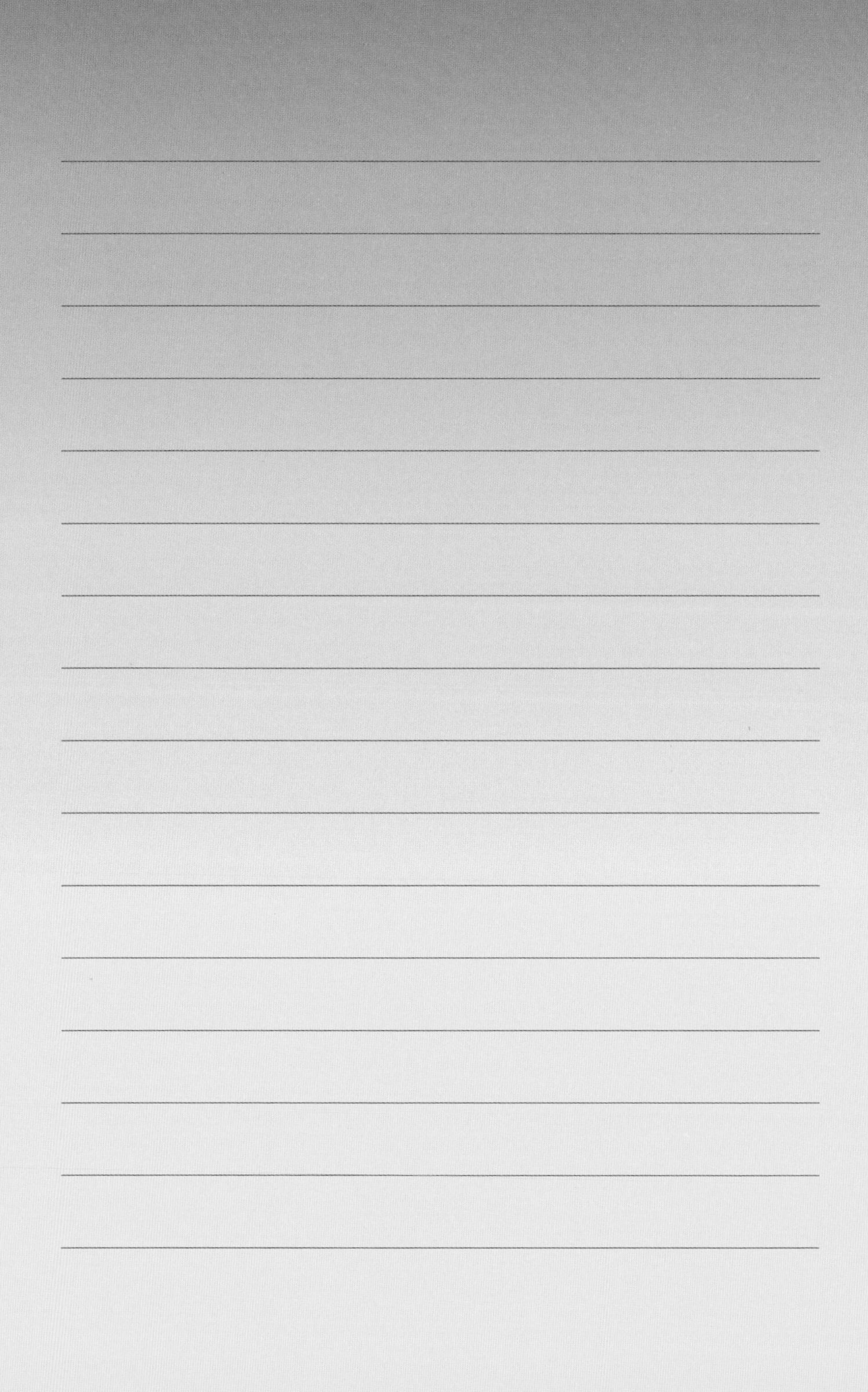

PROGRESS OVER PERFECT

THE BEGINNING

Fill in your journey of tiny progress that has gotten you to where you are today.

ON

Success doesn't always have to be about giant, shareable accomplishments. It can be small, private victories known by you alone.

WHERE
I AM
TODAY

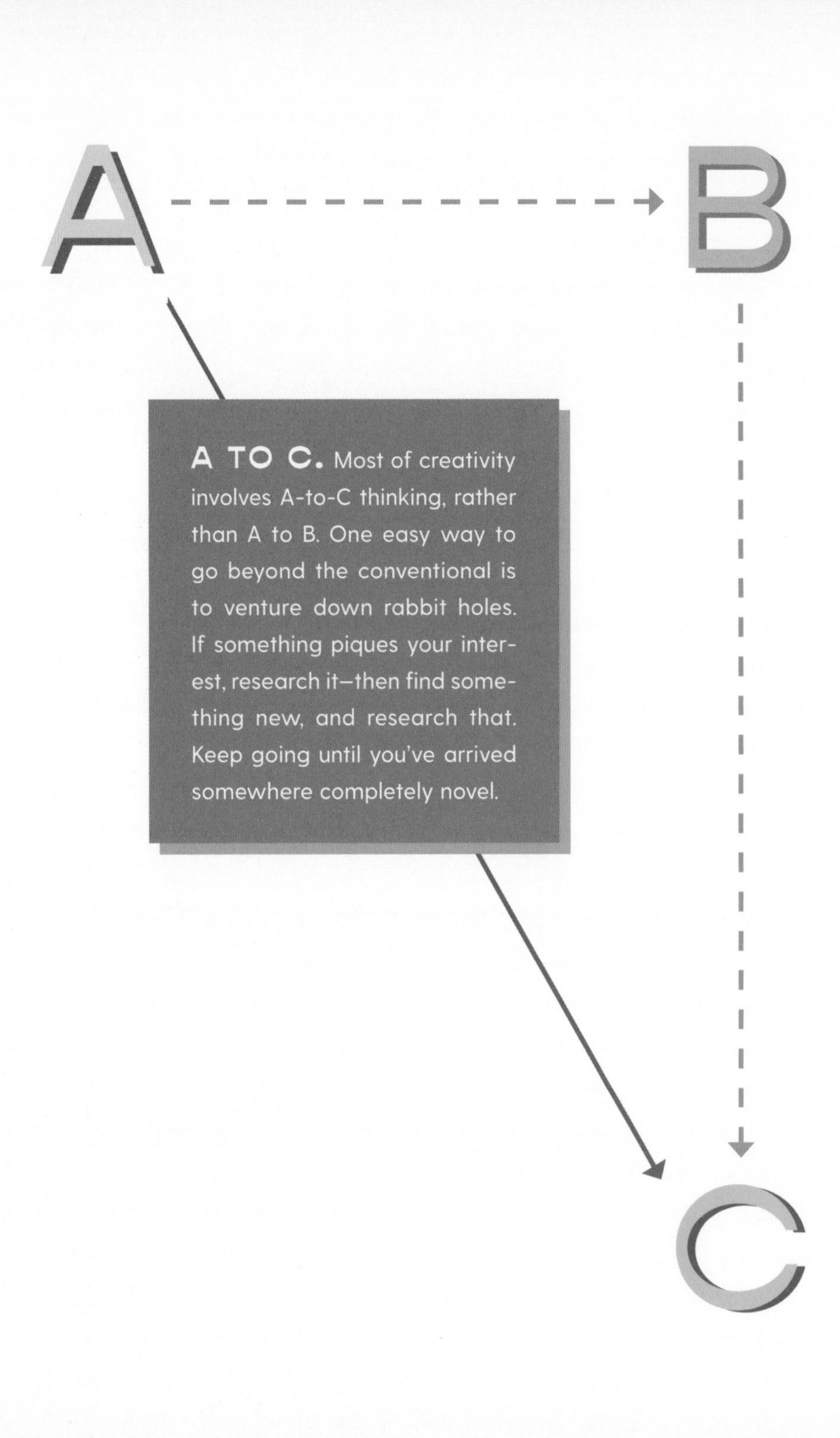

A TO C. Most of creativity involves A-to-C thinking, rather than A to B. One easy way to go beyond the conventional is to venture down rabbit holes. If something piques your interest, research it—then find something new, and research that. Keep going until you've arrived somewhere completely novel.

AGAIN, BEGIN.

As an English teacher in South Korea, the phrase I used the most was "다시 시작" (dasi sijag) which translates to "again, begin." When you're learning something new, you will always make mistakes, but you can't let yourself get stuck in the mistake. Acknowledge the mistake, pick yourself up, and again, begin.

What do you need to pick up again? Is it an abandoned art project? A forgotten friendship? A dream deferred? You can do it. 다시 시작.

ALL YOUR IDEAS. In the notes section of my phone, I have a note called "truly all of my ideas." It's the place where I jot down passing thoughts that seem interesting (short story ideas, restaurants I would open, art projects that would be fun). I often go back to it when I'm feeling stuck—and I find that I always feel more creative after seeing that I do, in fact, have lots of good ideas.

WRITE YOUR IDEAS HERE, OR START A NOTE IN YOUR PHONE. THEY DON'T HAVE TO BE PRACTICAL—DREAM BIG!

In the arena

An invader has come
to prevail upon my brain
to tell me what and why
  I'm doing wrong
and I listen
before I even think to ask
and who are you?

TO-WRITE LIST. Jot down things you want to write. They can be anything: letters, short stories, screenplays, novels, essays, recipes, or even funny tweets.

AND THEN KEEP GOING IF YOU'RE FEELING INSPIRED!

START WITH FIVE ITEMS

COZY CONTENT. We all have our staple movies or TV shows that we rewatch. Write down your go-tos and your reason for turning to them, so you can always find the right one to get reinspired.

MOVIE/SHOW:	REASON I WATCH:

BOOKS THAT MAKE ME FEEL ALIVE. For me, this is a lot of dystopian novels and Jane Austen. Weird combo, but to each their own! Draw and illustrate the spines of your favorite books, so you can turn to your virtual bookshelf and feel joy.

Create,

on't Hate
COLOR
ME IN!

WORK IN PROGRESS.
Creativity is a muscle, not a talent. Draw an object in front of you three different times.

DON'T JUDGE YOURSELF; JUST COMMIT TO THE PROCESS OF MAKING PROGRESS.

GET PROFESSIONAL. Both professional and amateur writers possess talent; the only difference between the two is skill. Skill is something you learn, practice, and continually improve. Do you have a talent that you need to practice? How will you continue to improve your skill?

THE CAT. You know the phrase “curiosity killed the cat,” but did you know that the rest of the phrase is “but satisfaction brought it back”? What’s something you were told not to be curious about? How can you reclaim your curiosity?

TIME CAPSULE

Nothing in life is permanent. You won't always have the same stresses or worries. Collect any random bits and bobs from today (receipts, ticket stubs, notes), and tape them below. Next, write down your to-do list or your worry list for the day. Look back on this page in a few weeks or months. How has your life changed? Do you have any new perspectives?

Draw a very rough doodle of your desk right now.

Color ME BLUE

Assign colors to your three most prominent emotions.

EMOTION:

EMOTION:

EMOTION:

MEMORY LANE. Write the funniest story you can remember from your teenage years.

The Funniest story from my teenage years

YOUR LIFE STORY

Write some titles for the stand-up special, memoir, or biopic of your life. Mine would be, *I Want a Snack, But I'm Not Hungry: A Memoir.*

ALTERNATE REALITY.

What's a nickname you wish you had had growing up?

ME ★ FOR ★ PRESIDENT

If you were running for president, what would your slogan be?

DRAW A SELF-PORTRAIT. It will be bad for 99 percent of us, but it will be 100 percent funny.

DRAW YOUR FAVORITE FLOWER. If you don't have a favorite flower, spend some time searching for them online, and pick one today!

YOU CAN'T FAIL IF YOU KEEP SHOWING UP.

STAY CURIOUS. Curiosity starts with a question and ends with a "there's so much more to learn." If you are stuck, it's often because you've stopped being curious. Research something from your "things to investigate list" (turn back to "The Cat;" your list is there), and write down what you find and your next step.

WRITER'S BLOCK. Finish these sentences to get your mind going.

I'VE ALWAYS WANTED TO:

THE SUMMER ALWAYS REMINDS ME OF:

IF FRIENDSHIP WERE A SONG, IT WOULD BE:

I WAS SURPRISED WHEN MY FIFTEEN-YEAR-OLD SELF RETURNED TO ME AND SAID:

THE MONTAGE. My favorite part of every movie is what I call the "eff-you montage," in which the protagonist defies the naysayers in their life and gets down to business. (i.e., the training montage in *Rocky II* or the "watch me shine" montage in *Legally Blonde*). List five scenes that would be in your montage (bonus points for a kick-ass song that goes with it).

1. ______________________________

____

2. ______________________________

____

3. ______________________________

____

4. ______________________________

____

5. ______________________________

____

Progress is
a horseshoe

WHERE ARE YOU MAKING PROGRESS?

LET YOUR MIND BE FREE.
I have ADHD, so most of the time, it feels like I'm actively fighting my brain for control. But every once in a while, I let my ADHD run the show. My brain hops from one idea to the next at whatever speed it chooses, and it expresses my feelings however it wants. This is especially true in my journal. I write my monthly budgets next to poems and grocery lists, next to ideas for movies. Organization is highly overvalued when it comes to creativity and inspiration. On the following two pages, let your mind run free, leave order at the door, and let your brain explore.

STUFF
NO.
hat you love.
JOY

RELATION-
SHIPS

FINDING INSPIRATION

is not entirely a solo endeavor. Part of the richness of life comes from the eclectic tapestry of friends and family we create to love and support us. It is our job to nurture those relationships and make sure they remain positive forces in our life. It is also our job to protect ourselves from negativity and toxicity by creating boundaries. This section addresses both sides of the relationship coin, positive and negative, in the hopes of creating a space for only good energies.

THE GAYLE TO YOUR OPRAH. Tape in or draw a picture here of your biggest cheerleader. It can be your partner, your best friend, your mom, or your cat. Sometimes it's just nice to remember that someone believes in you.

______________________________ **believes in me!**

[name]

LISTEN FOR INSPIRATION.

I find listening to be the most inspiring thing we can do. Ask a friend, a coworker, or even a stranger an unexpected question today. For example: If you could live in another country, which one would it be? Or, what's the song you've listened to most in your life? Which do you prefer: mountains, beach, or desert?

WHO DO YOU

I often draw my strength from the women who came before me. Mindy Kaling, Nora Ephron, Oprah Winfrey, Barbra Streisand, Lucille Ball, and my

CARRY WITH YOU?

mother, Cookie Santiago Perez. Who do you carry with you to give you strength? Paste in or draw the people in your inspirational wallet.

OLD FRIENDS. Whenever I'm feeling down or lonely, I go back to a list of people I miss, and I reach out to them. You can do it via text, call, or snail mail. It's just nice to remember there are people outside your immediate sphere who love you. Make that list here.

MOST INSPIRING PEOPLE LIST. Who are the people who you want to be when you "grow up"? They don't have to be famous. (In other words, "Dad" is a totally great answer!)

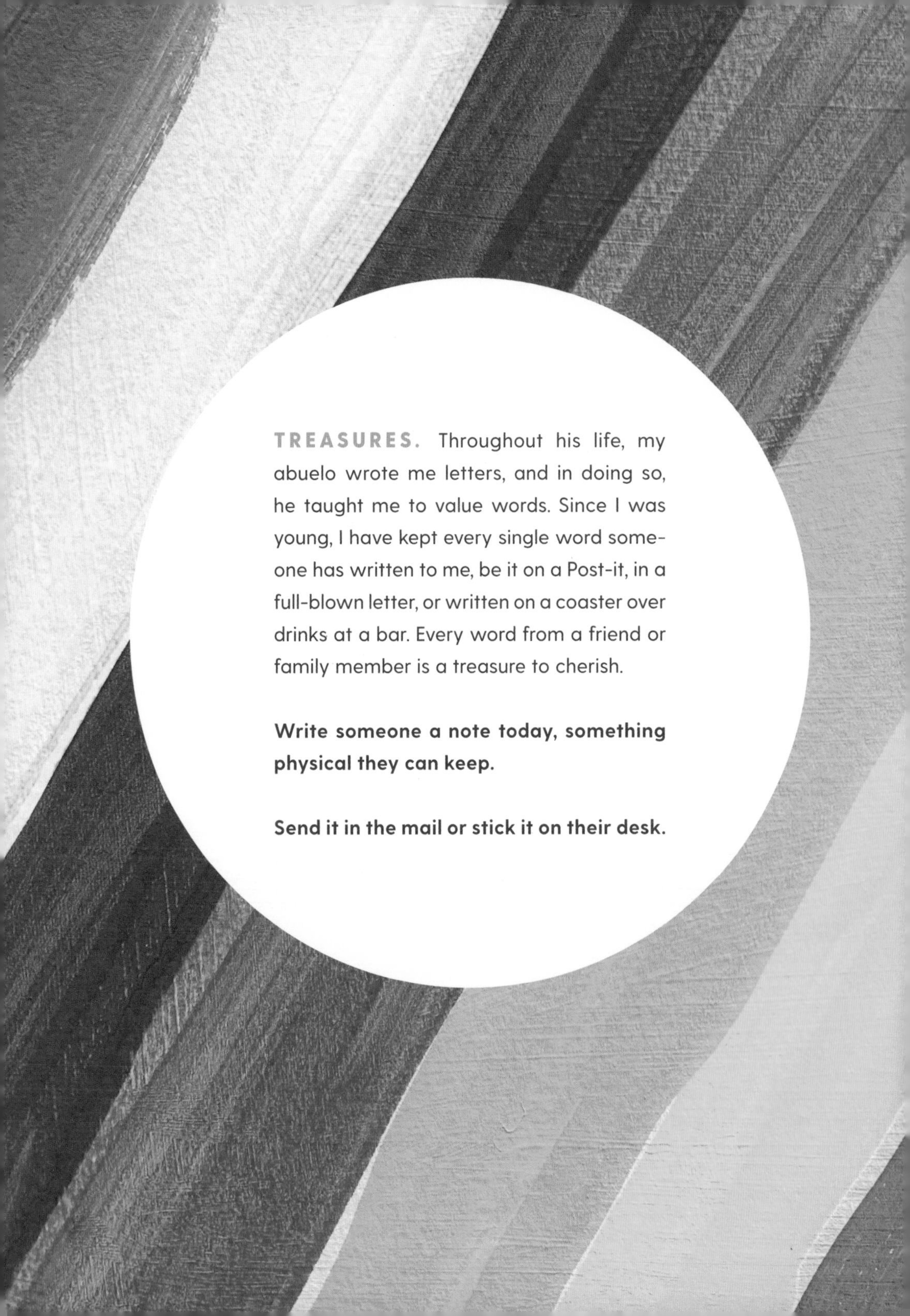

TREASURES. Throughout his life, my abuelo wrote me letters, and in doing so, he taught me to value words. Since I was young, I have kept every single word someone has written to me, be it on a Post-it, in a full-blown letter, or written on a coaster over drinks at a bar. Every word from a friend or family member is a treasure to cherish.

Write someone a note today, something physical they can keep.

Send it in the mail or stick it on their desk.

THAT WHICH YOU'VE GIVEN AWAY. Ironically, we tend to feel the most grateful for what we have when we give to others. One of my favorite quotes is from a sign hanging in the background of George Bailey's bank in *It's a Wonderful Life*: "All you can take with you is that which you've given away." What do you have to give to others?

A FRIEND TO ALL IS A FRIEND TO NONE. People-pleasing often does nothing but create resentment because we aren't speaking our mind or standing our ground. Where you think you are being considerate, you are actually hurting both your integrity and the integrity of the relationship by not being honest. What are the scenarios in your life in which you find yourself people-pleasing the most? Write down three situations in which you found yourself engaging in people-pleasing. Then write down what you actually wanted from the situation instead.

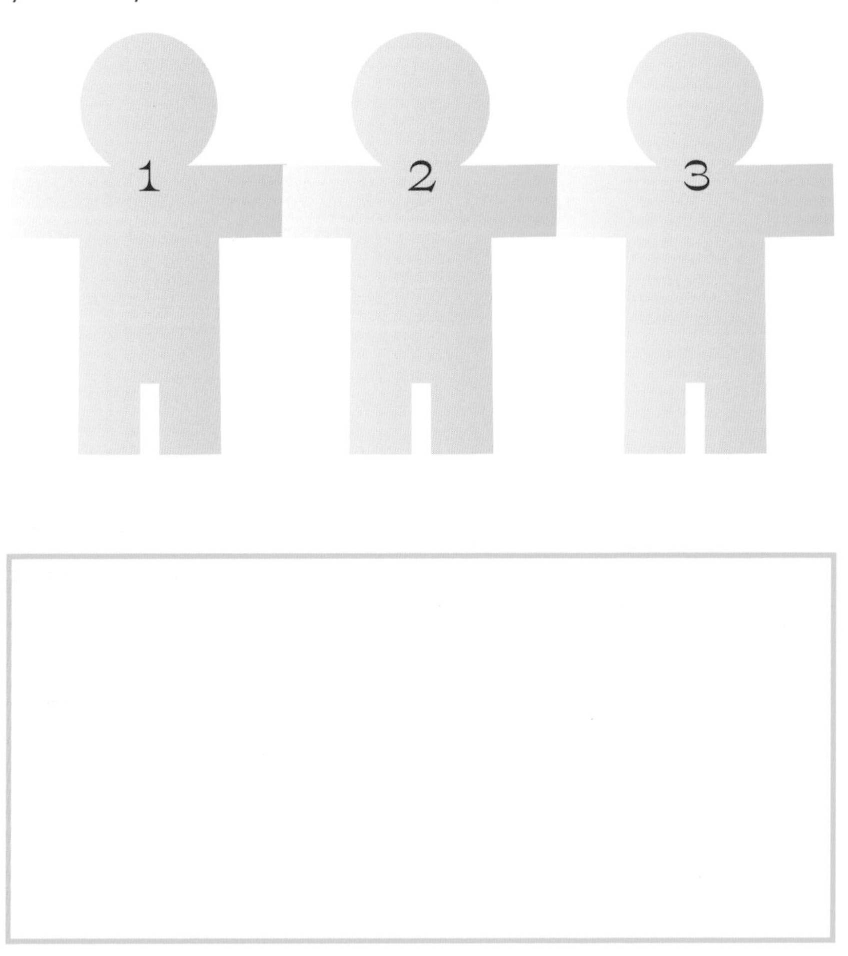

BOUNDARIES CREATE EMPATHY.

This may seem counterintuitive, but setting boundaries is actually one of the best ways we can create space for understanding one another. Dr. Brené Brown's advice for how to do this is simple. She says, "Choose discomfort over resentment." In other words, it's not rude or selfish to set boundaries.

In what relationship or scenario do you need to create boundaries?

____

____

____

____

SUPPORTING

We may be the main characters in our own lives, but remember, we're also the supporting characters in the lives of others. Take this role seriously, and help others find their purpose.

CHARACTERS

SHARE THE SPOTLIGHT. Sometimes we get bogged down because we're so concerned with our own goals and achievements. Who are three people who deserve hype in your life? Text each one of them something encouraging and true about them right now.

A LITTLE HELP FROM MY FRIENDS. Kindness can both make and break our days. What are some random acts of kindness you've encountered lately?

What are some kindnesses you can extend to others?

DON'T WASTE IT.

We're here for such a short time. Don't waste it on regret and grudges. What grudge do you need to let go of in order to move on?

DON'T TAKE IT PERSON-ALLY.

In *The Four Agreements*, Don Miguel Ruiz says, "Don't take anything personally." People do things because of themselves, not because of you. What are you taking personally that you can free yourself from?

SEEING THE TRUTH. Who in your life really sees you for you? What is it that they see? Draw three self-portraits that show how the people who love you see you.

How ________________ **sees me.**
[name]

How ________________ **sees me.**
[name]

How ________________ **sees me.**
[name]

EM-
POWE
MENT

R-

INSPIRATION IS BUILT ON A foundation of self-care. Like Maslow's hierarchy of needs, if we don't first tend to our base needs as a human (water, shelter, safety, love), then we can never become self-actualized people. This section is about taking care of those needs, and in doing so, empowering yourself to take on whatever it is you feel is your personal mission in this world. In taking care of ourselves, we are actually creating space to take care of others.

What to make?

what do you want to make?
 she whispered into my ear.
inspiration.
 I don't know, I replied.
make something to comfort your own soul
 that's what the whole world needs.
people making things to heal themselves.

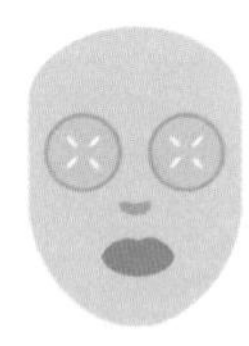

PUT YOURSELF FIRST. Self-care is about putting yourself first, so you can help those around you. It's like airplane safety. You put on your oxygen mask first so you can breathe and more effectively help those around you.

List an activity or part of your life where you are not putting yourself first.

List a way you can actively change that today. What has to change to put yourself first?

WHAT IS YOUR NOURISHMENT?
We have to nourish ourselves to feel fulfilled. Just like my houseplant, whose leaves wither without water, you, too, need sustenance. What nourishes you? What are you missing?

WHAT IS YOUR

MANTRA?

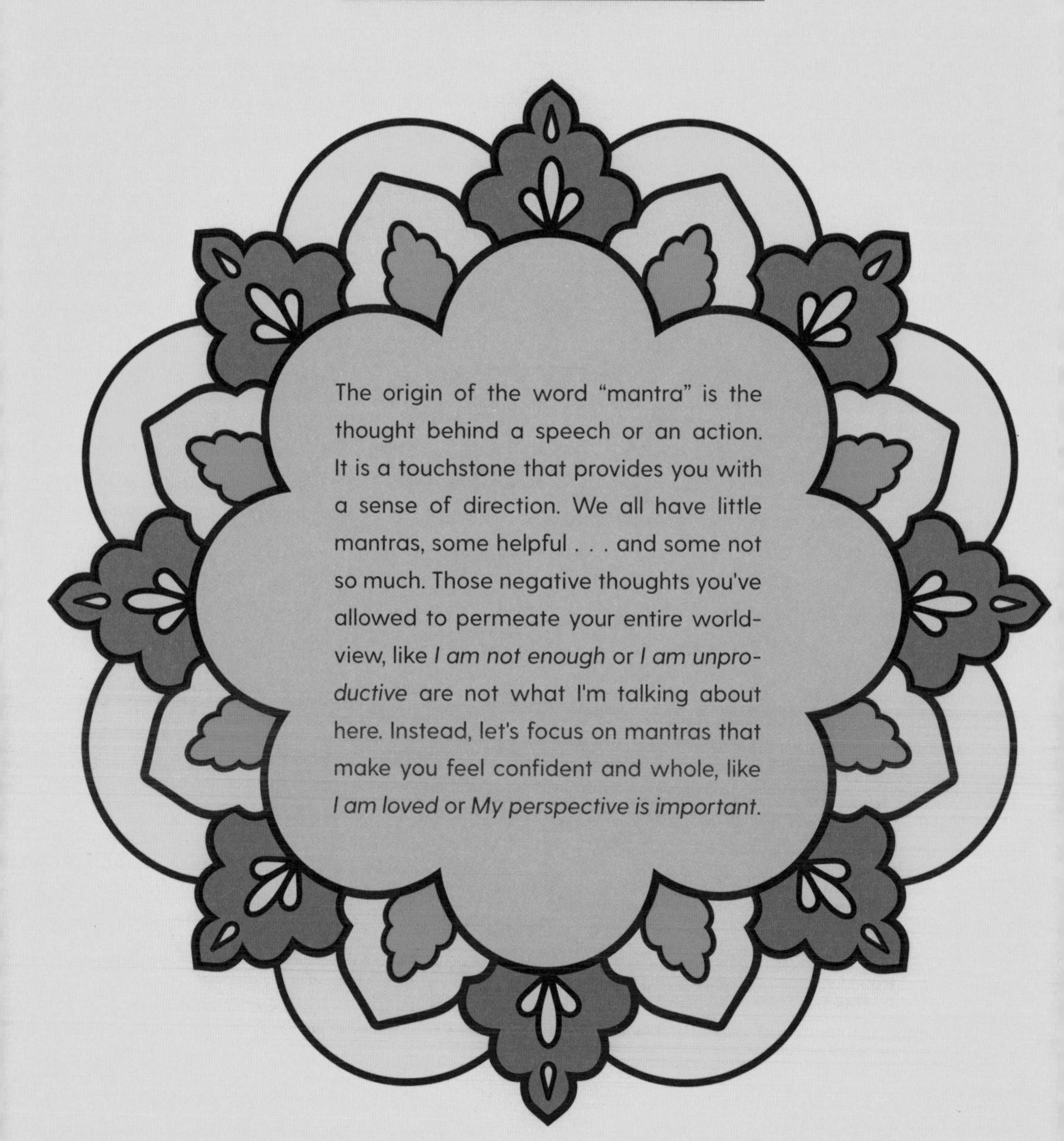

The origin of the word "mantra" is the thought behind a speech or an action. It is a touchstone that provides you with a sense of direction. We all have little mantras, some helpful . . . and some not so much. Those negative thoughts you've allowed to permeate your entire worldview, like *I am not enough* or *I am unproductive* are not what I'm talking about here. Instead, let's focus on mantras that make you feel confident and whole, like *I am loved* or *My perspective is important*.

Write down your favorite positive mantra, and look back on it whenever you're feeling down.

ENERGY CHECK.

We only have so much energy each day. Is there something or someone who is sapping your energy? If so, how can you rid yourself of the bad vibes?

What or who gives you energy? How can you amplify it?

GET INTO YOUR SENSES. A quick stress check for when you're feeling anxious or overwhelmed is to connect with your body. Get out of your head and into your senses.

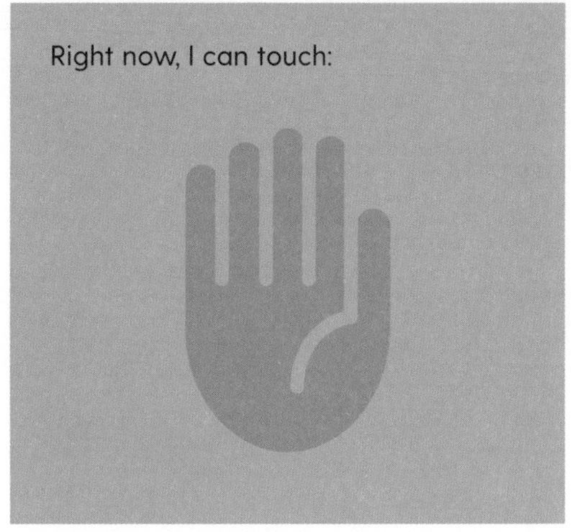

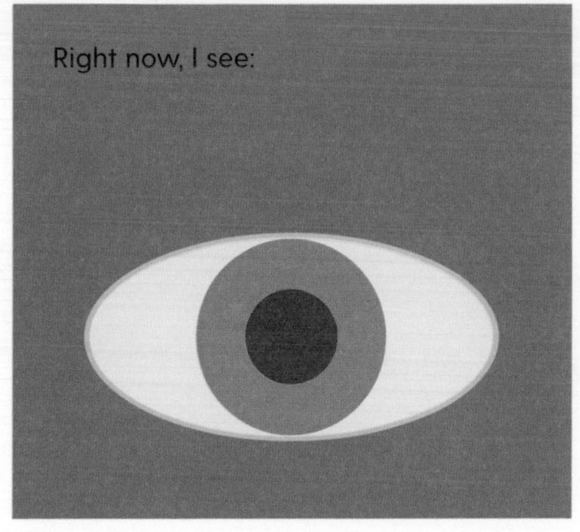

Make a list of habits you have that are beneficial for your mental health.

THE GOOD STUFF

Make a list of habits you want to add.

OH, THE PLACES YOU'LL GO. Travel is my favorite way to get out of a rut. But even when you can't physically go to a new place, you can always mentally go somewhere new. There are lots of ways to take a mental vacation (listen to playlists that sound like the places you want to go, watch YouTube videos of that destination). Write out an itinerary for your dream vacation. Be specific, and include what you want to see, feel, eat, and experience.

Destination:

A Comparison Poem

I never met a daisy
worried that it should be
  a rose
and yet here I am

PATIENCE IS A PROCESS. Good tea needs time to brew in order to release its aromas. What is an area of your life that you've been impatient with? What will you gain by allowing yourself time to slow down?

THE ULTIMATE LIST

What ten things are on your bucket list? Refer to it when you're feeling lost.

✲ ____________________

✲ ____________________

✲ ____________________

✲ ____________________

✲ ____________________

✲ ____________________

✲ ____________________

✲ ____________________

✲ ____________________

✲ ____________________

THE "HOW I WANT TO LIVE MY LIFE" LIST.

Unlike a bucket list, this one doesn't have to be a lifelong to-do list. It can be something like "saying what I think when I mean it" or "waking up and watching the sunrise every day for a week."

UNPLUG. In a TED Talk, author Anne Lamott said, "Almost everything will work again if you unplug it for a few minutes, including you." Burnout is the enemy of inspiration.

don't take yourself too seriously

Work hard, but don't take yourself too seriously. Even though you're an adult, you deserve to play and feel as much joy as any carefree kid. Your gift as a human is to experience, not do. Do something today that is just for fun.

FIND YOUR HAPPY PLACE. Once, in the middle of a panic attack, my girlfriend stopped me, looked me in the eye, and said, "Why don't you go draw a bath and watch *Little Women*?" I did, and my panic almost immediately subsided. It's not just because I love listening to Jo rant about sisterhood while I'm in the tub, but also because practicing self-care teaches you how to self-soothe. If you're having a rough time of it, your happy place will rescue you.

What's something that immediately calms you down? (Some ideas: a specific candle or scent, a song, a movie)

Where is your happy place?

What activity makes you feel most relaxed? (Some ideas: walking, napping, reading, painting, playing Candy Crush)

LESS IS MORE. What is creating clutter in your life? What things can you clear out to make space for the good stuff?

PENCILS UP. Draw how you're feeling right now in this moment.

NEW HABITS. According to research, it is much easier to start a new habit if you attach it to an old one. For example: If you want to start listening to the news every morning, start by doing it every time you brush your teeth.

Look back at the new habits you want to form (you created it under "The Good Stuff" a few pages ago). What old habits can you attach to them?

RITUAL OVER ROUTINE. The difference between routine and ritual is intention. Write down your ideal morning and nighttime rituals that would help add clarity and space to the beginning and end of every day.

LIKE THE PLAGUE. We all tend to avoid hard truths and painful insecurities in our life. For some people, it's through exercise; for others, it's eating junk food or keeping busy. But avoidance means that we aren't confronting or working through the issues. Avoidance means dooming ourselves to staying stuck. What is a hard truth you are not confronting in your life? How are you avoiding it?

HARD TRUTH

HARD TRUTH

HEALING COMES
FROM FEELING.
TRY TO ADDRESS
YOUR PAIN
HEAD-ON.

NOTICING. The first step to being more present in your life starts with paying attention. Make ten observations about what is around you right now. The last few might be tough, but don't stop short.

CHECK YOUR WORRY.

Worrying is the antithesis of action. Draw the worries you carry with you, and leave them all outside the door.

FREE
SPACE

BINGO

BITS, BOBS, AND THOUGHTS. Use this space however your brain sees fit: to-do lists, tic-tac-toe, math homework, or doddles—these pages are your oyster!

ACKNOWLEDGMENTS

To the Potter team: Thank you to my editor, Gabbie Van Tassel, for being on the *For Inspiration* journey with me from day one. Thank you to Amelia Iuvino and Terry Deal for copyediting this book. Thank you to Kelli Tokos for handling all the production management. Thank you to Lise Sukhu and Danielle Deschenes for your beautiful designs.

To my team: Thank you to Eve Attermann, Haley Heidemann, and Sam Birmingham, y'all know books and you know me, which is all I could ever ask for. Thank you to Chelsea Dern for inspiring me in all my other writing. Thank you to Carolyn Moneta for being my ride or die. Thank you to Travis Dunlap for making *Listen to This for Inspiration* happen. Thank you to Luke Dillion and Greg Walter for fitting all the pieces of my career together.

To my friends and family: Thank you to my family for always and forever giving me a place to rest. Thank you to all of my group chats that give me life and laughter. CLAM, Wanna Be on Top? Gaylor Swift. Thank you to all the people who have helped and inspired my creativity. Most recently: Chantel Houston, Amanda Holland, Kirsten King, Casey Rackham, Madeline Hendricks, Resheida Brady, Cristian Martinez, Nicole Paulhus, Kyle Hanagami, Quinta Brunson, Kate Peterman, Jennie Urman, Vanessa Magos, Kate Pauley, Andrew Gauthier, Andrew Shearer.

Thank you to my bean for being my favorite person. I love you.

Thank you to James, my cat, and Laurie, my future cat.

Published in the United States by Clarkson Potter/Publishers, an imprint of Random House, a division of Penguin Random House LLC, New York.

clarksonpotter.com

CLARKSON POTTER is a trademark and POTTER with colophon is a registered trademark of Penguin Random House LLC.

Some illustrations were originally published in Read This for Inspiration (Clarkson Potter, 2020).

ISBN 978-0-593-13536-5

Printed in China

Illustrators: Jen B. Peters, Sarah Walsh, Marisol Ortega, Olivia Herrick, Lise Sukhu, and Danielle Deschenes

Additional credits: tiger pouncing © CSA Images/Getty Images

Editor: Gabrielle Van Tassel
Designers: Lise Sukhu, Danielle Deschenes, and Laura Palese
Production Editor: Terry Deal
Production Manager: Kelli Tokos
Copy Editor: Amelia Ayrelan Iuvino

10 9 8 7 6 5 4 3 2 1

First Edition